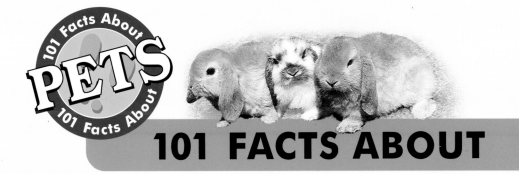

101 Facts About PETS
101 Facts About

101 FACTS ABOUT

RABBITS

Please visit our web site at: www.garethstevens.com
For a free color catalog describing Gareth Stevens Publishing's list of high-quality books and multimedia programs, call 1-800-542-2595 (USA) or 1-800-461-9120 (Canada). Gareth Stevens Publishing's Fax: (414) 332-3567.

Library of Congress Cataloging-in-Publication Data

Barnes, Julia, 1955-
    101 facts about rabbits / by Julia Barnes. — North American ed.
      p. cm. — (101 facts about pets)
    Includes bibliographical references and index.
    ISBN 0-8368-2891-7 (lib. bdg.)
    1. Rabbits—Miscellanea—Juvenile literature. 2. Rabbits—Behavior—Miscellanea—
Juvenile literature. [1. Rabbits—Miscellanea. 2. Rabbits as pets—Miscellanea.]
    I. Title: One hundred one facts about rabbits. II. Title. III. Series.
    SF453.2.B37   2001
    636.9'322—dc21   2001031056

This North American edition first published in 2001 by
Gareth Stevens Publishing
A World Almanac Education Group Company
330 West Olive Street, Suite 100
Milwaukee, WI 53212 USA

This U.S. edition © 2001 by Gareth Stevens, Inc. Original edition © 2001 by Ringpress Books Limited. First published by Ringpress Books Limited, P.O. Box 8, Lydney, Gloucestershire, GL15 4YN, United Kingdom. Additional end matter © 2001 by Gareth Stevens, Inc.

Ringpress Series Editor: Claire Horton-Bussey
Ringpress Designer: Sara Howell
Gareth Stevens Editor: Heidi Sjostrom

Printed in Hong Kong through Printworks Int. Ltd.

1 2 3 4 5 6 7 8 9 05 04 03 02 01

101 FACTS ABOUT

RABBITS

Julia Barnes

Gareth Stevens Publishing
A WORLD ALMANAC EDUCATION GROUP COMPANY

1 Rabbits have hopped on Earth a long time. They were seen in Portugal and Spain more than 3,000 years ago. Rabbits also appear in Stone Age cave paintings.

2 About 2,000 years ago, Romans raised rabbits for meat and fur. They kept the rabbits in large, stone-walled pens called leporaria.

3 People started keeping rabbits as pets only a little more than 200 years ago. Now rabbits are one of the most popular small animals to have as pets.

4 Rabbits belong to the *Lagomorpha* family. They look a lot like rodents, such as rats, mice, hamsters, and guinea pigs. Scientific studies, however, have shown that rabbits might be more closely related to hoofed animals, such as horses.

5 Hares are rabbits' closest relatives, but rabbits and hares are not exactly alike. Newborn rabbits are hairless and helpless. Newborn hares have fur and can see and hop almost immediately. Hares are much faster than rabbits, too.

6 "Rabbit" comes from "rabet," an old English word that means "groove." "Rabbit" may mean "burrow-digger." "Bunny" comes from "bun," which, in parts of England, means "squirrel."

7 In Europe, wild rabbits dig connected burrows, called warrens, to live in.

10 Wild rabbits sleep a lot during the day, then come out at sunset to eat grass and other plants.

11 Three rabbits can eat as much grass in a day as one sheep. Rabbits can be a serious problem for farmers.

8 In North America, wild rabbits dig shallow holes, instead of burrows, or use the burrows of other animals.

9 Most of the wild rabbits in North America are Cottontails, named for the white fur on their tails.

6

12 Rabbits are excellent pets for children. They are gentle animals that are easy to handle and take care of, and they can live outdoors in **hutches**.

13 Most pet rabbits will live five to ten years, but some have lived longer.

14 The oldest rabbit on record is Flopsy, a wild rabbit that was caught in Tasmania, Australia. Flopsy was kept as a pet until it died at the age of 18 years and 11 months.

15 All pet rabbits are **descendants** of the European wild rabbit.

16 Special **breeding** has produced about 45 different kinds of rabbits, from Flemish Giants to Mini Lops, in 80 color varieties, including red, silver, and lilac.

17 Rabbits range in size from giant breeds to dwarf breeds. Giant Chinchillas weigh about 14 pounds (6.5 kilograms), Netherland Dwarfs (below), about 2 pounds (0.9 kg). American Sables weigh 8 to 9 pounds (3.5 to 4 kg).

18 Nearly all pet rabbits, including most dwarf breeds, are bigger than their wild ancestors.

19 The fur of pet rabbits can be one of four main types: satin, rex, angora, and normal.

20 Satin fur is thick, shiny, and lies flat. Rabbit breeds with satin fur include Satins, Mini Satins, and Satin Angoras.

21 Rex fur is short and stands up like velvet. The Rex and Velveteen Lop breeds have this kind of fur.

23 Normal fur, which is like the hair on a wild rabbit, is about 1 inch (2.5 cm) long. The Havana (below), Chinchilla (below), and New Zealand breeds are among the many types of rabbits with normal fur.

22 Angora fur is very fluffy and more than 1¼ inches (3 centimeters) long. Giant Angoras (above) and American Fuzzy Lops have this soft, "fancy breed" fur.

▲ Chinchilla

Havana ▶

measured from the tip of one ear to the tip of the other ear, can be 28 inches (71 cm) long. This rabbit needs a large living space to help keep it from stepping on its sensitive ears.

24 Some rabbit breeds have drooping ears. These rabbits are known as "lops." Lop breeds include the Dwarf Lop (above), which is a very popular pet.

26 Rabbits come in many different colors. Wild rabbits are a color called **agouti**. On pet breeds, this color is called chestnut.

25 The ears of an English Lop are very delicate and, when

27 Pet rabbits can also have fur that is red, black, white, blue, chocolate, lilac, gold, silver, copper, gray, or a mixture of colors.

breed to breed. Some breeds do not make good pets.

30 The best pet rabbits include the lively Dutch, one of the oldest known breeds, and the Himalayan, which is slightly smaller and calmer.

28 Rabbits can have beautiful markings. Sealpoint markings are like those on a Siamese cat. Dalmatian markings are blotches of color on a white body. The Harlequin breed (above) has a patchwork of black, orange, and fawn.

29 The personalities, or temperaments, of rabbits can be different from

11

31 Angoras are not the best pets because they need grooming so often. Britannia Petites can have nasty tempers, so they are poor choices as pets, too.

32 A **crossbred** rabbit can be a good pet, but, if you buy the rabbit when it is a baby, you will not know how big it will be when full grown or what its personality will be like.

33 Buy a rabbit when it is about eight weeks old, so it gets used to being handled while it is young.

34 The best place to buy rabbits is at a good pet store that has an experienced staff to help you. If you want rabbits for shows, however, rabbits from a pet store will not do. You will need to find a breeder who specializes in producing **purebred/pedigree** rabbits.

35 To tell if a rabbit is healthy, look for the following signs:

- a rounded body with no unusual swellings
- a full coat of fur without **mats** or dirt
- bright, clear eyes that are not red or watery
- a clean, wiggling nose with no **discharge**
- clean ears that have no wax buildup, discharge, or redness, and have ear flaps that are not damaged
- teeth that are not broken or overgrown (Drooling can be a sign of tooth trouble.)
- quiet, regular breathing

36 Rabbits do not always get along well with each other. Two males are likely to fight.

37 A male and a female will get along fine – but they will produce lots of babies!

38 A male rabbit is a "buck." A female is a "doe." You can ask an experienced rabbit-keeper how to tell the difference.

39 Pet rabbits are often kept indoors and are trained to be house rabbits. If you prefer, you can keep your rabbit outside in a hutch.

40 The size of a hutch will depend on the kind of rabbit that will live in it. The hutch should be at least 9 inches (23 cm) off the ground to avoid dampness.

41 A hutch should have a separate sleeping area for the rabbit. It should also have a secure wire front to keep out rats and mice.

42 Keep the hutch warm. Rabbits can get sick at temperatures that are below 55° Fahrenheit (12.8° Celsius).

44 An indoor rabbit needs a large wire cage with a board covering the wire floor to protect the rabbit's feet. Shredded paper is good bedding material and the most convenient to use.

45 Both a hutch and a cage must have a supply of fresh water. A water bottle from a pet store makes providing water easy.

43 Rabbits like a nice, deep bed. Put a thick layer of straw or wood shavings into the hutch, along with some fresh green hay for the rabbit to eat or sleep on.

46 In nice weather, rabbits like to be outdoors in an exercise run.

47 The run should be as big as possible, and it must be shaded from direct sunlight. Be sure that a water bottle is attached to the side of the run.

48 You can construct a maze in the run with some lengths of pipe. Your rabbit will enjoy tunneling in and out.

49 Rabbit-proofing your house is important if your pet rabbit is allowed to run free in certain rooms. Electrical cords and many houseplants are especially dangerous for your rabbit.

50 All rabbits love to **gnaw** and chew, so make sure your rabbit cannot damage furniture.

jump up on. If you cut doors and windows in empty cardboard boxes, your rabbit will hop in and out of them.

51 A house rabbit should have its own cushion to sit on, or you can cover a furniture cushion with old fabric or towels to keep the rabbit from damaging it.

52 Like most house pets, rabbits like to play with toys, especially balls that they can push and roll. They also like things to

53 In the wild, rabbits have toilet areas, so it is not difficult to train a rabbit to use a litter box. Be patient and never yell at the rabbit for making a mistake.

17

54 Rabbits have a very good sense of taste. A rabbit has 17,000 taste buds in its mouth. A person has only 10,000 taste buds.

55 A wild rabbit eats a wide variety of vegetables and other plants. A pet rabbit, however, should eat pellets purchased from a pet store. They are made specially to give pet rabbits a complete diet.

56 Pet rabbits must eat hay, too. Grass hay, such as timothy hay, is best. Besides being healthy food, hay helps control hair balls.

57 Your rabbit will also enjoy fresh foods, such as carrots, broccoli, parsley, alfalfa sprouts, and green leaf lettuce.

60 When you first bring your rabbit home, give it a chance to settle in. Watching how it behaves will help you understand it.

61 Rabbits can move their ears in every direction, and they are very sensitive to sound. Try not to make sudden noises that will frighten your rabbit.

58 Avoid iceberg head lettuce. It has very little food value, and too much of it causes **diarrhea**.

59 Do not leave food lying around in the hutch or cage. Rotting food can cause serious illness.

19

62 Rabbits can see to the front, to the sides, and to the back. This range of vision is important for spotting enemies. Up close, however, rabbits have poor eyesight. Do not be surprised if your rabbit fails to spot objects right near it.

63 A rabbit's sense of touch comes from its whiskers, which are as long as its body is wide. A rabbit's whiskers help it find its way in the dark and measure the width of places it wants to crawl into.

64 When you see a rabbit rubbing its chin against objects, it is marking territory with its scent. Humans are not able to smell this scent.

65 In the mornings, you might see your rabbit eating its droppings.

This is not a bad habit. A rabbit needs the light-colored droppings it passes at night to help digest its food.

66 In the wild, rabbits warn each other of approaching danger by thumping their back feet. A pet rabbit might thump if it is frightened. A bossy rabbit might do it as a threat.

67 To avoid being seen by enemies, rabbits will lie flat on the ground. If you see a rabbit lying flat, it is probably very frightened.

68 If a rabbit is sitting up on its **haunches**, it is probably trying to get a better view, sniff out a scent, or reach a tempting treat.

69 Rabbits will often make sounds to communicate their feelings. A rabbit that mutters, making a short, scolding sound, is angry or is giving a warning.

70 A rabbit's hissing sounds a lot like a cat's hissing. It is a sign of **aggression**. A hissing rabbit might be ready to attack.

71 A content rabbit will softly grind its teeth. You might hear this grinding when you pet your rabbit.

72 When a rabbit makes a loud squeal, it is either in great danger or in terrible pain.

73 The more you pet and handle your rabbit, the more tame it will become. Hand-feeding is a good way to make friends.

74 Rabbits are nervous animals, so always handle your pet rabbit firmly, but gently.

up your rabbit, sit on the floor, in case you drop it, or it hops suddenly out of your hands.

76 A safe way to hold a rabbit is to have it facing away from you with one of your hands under its front legs and the other hand holding its rear end.

75 Never lift a rabbit by its ears! The right way to pick up a rabbit is to take hold of the loose skin at the back of its neck with one hand and support its rear end and hind legs with the other. The first time you try to pick

77 With lots of food treats and lots of patience, you can train your rabbit to respond to spoken commands.

78 With the commands "come," "go home," and "be clean," you can train your rabbit to come to you, to go back to its cage, and to use its litter box.

79 "No" is a command that is important to use with house rabbits. It will stop their bad behavior. Say "no" with a firm voice, and repeat this command every time your rabbit misbehaves. It will not take long for the rabbit to understand you.

80 Your rabbit will be a good pet if you give it healthy food, a clean place to live, and lots of attention.

81 A rabbit's hutch or cage should be kept clean at all times. Every day, you will have to remove wet bedding and the rabbit's droppings. You should also clean the feeding bowls and give the rabbit fresh water.

85 A rabbit is very uncomfortable when its front teeth get too long. If your rabbit drools or is having trouble eating, a veterinarian might have to cut back its teeth.

82 Every week, remove all the bedding and clean the cage thoroughly.

83 A rabbit's long, front teeth need care, too. Giving your pet rabbit hard foods to gnaw on helps.

84 In one year, your rabbit's front teeth, or incisors, could grow as much as 5 inches (12.7 cm).

86 Rabbits keep their nails trimmed by scratching and digging. If your rabbit's nails grow too long, the safest way to cut them back is to have a veterinarian clip them.

87 The amount of grooming a rabbit needs will depend on the length of its fur. Shorthaired rabbits (below) need brushing only when they are shedding fur, usually once or twice a year.

88 Longhaired rabbits, such as a Cashmere Lop (above), need brushing at least once a week.

89 Exotic Angora rabbits need constant grooming and special housing to keep their long, soft fur from getting dirty and matted.

90 An unhealthy rabbit might show some of the following signs:
- a dirty, matted coat
- runny eyes or nose
- discharge from the ears
- diarrhea
- drinking more – or less
- drooling or difficulty eating
- loss of appetite
- difficult or noisy breathing

If you notice any of these signs, consult a veterinarian.

91 If your rabbit eats normally but does not look healthy, it might have worms in its digestive system. Take the rabbit to a veterinarian for treatment.

92 Pet rabbits need **vaccinations** to prevent viral hemorrhagic disease and myxomatosis. Rabbits that get these diseases usually die. Ask a veterinarian for advice.

95 Most baby rabbits are born at night, about one month after their parents have mated.

93 Female rabbits can have babies at any time of the year. Wild rabbits often have many **litters** in a single year. Each litter has about five babies.

96 Rabbits are born without fur, and newborn rabbits cannot see, hear, or hop.

94 A male Norfolk Star rabbit named Chewer holds the record for producing the most young. Chewer fathered 40,000 offspring between 1968 and 1973.

100 When rabbits are two months old, they are completely independent and ready to go to new homes.

101 Rabbits are truly delightful pets. The more time you spend with your rabbit, the more you will enjoy owning one.

97 Within seven days, a baby rabbit starts to grow fur, and, by that time, its weight has doubled.

98 Baby rabbits open their eyes when they are about 10 days old. They can hear at 12 days.

99 At 18 days, they are eating solid food.

Glossary

aggression: an act of forceful or attacking behavior.

agouti: a grayish brown color of fur formed by alternate bands of gray, yellow, and black on each individual hair.

breeding: mating a male and a female of a species to produce a special variety of offspring.

crossbred: having parents that are each a different pedigree breed.

descendants: those born after any number of earlier generations in a certain family or species.

diarrhea: watery bowel movements that happen too often.

discharge: a thick or watery fluid that seeps through an opening.

gnaw: bite steadily on something and wear it away bit by bit.

haunches: parts of an animal's body that include the tops of the thighs, the hips, and the buttocks.

hutches: outdoor pens or cages for small animals, such as rabbits or guinea pigs.

Lagomorpha: the scientific name for a family of gnawing, plant-eating mammals that includes rabbits, hares, and pikas.

litters: groups of animals that are born at the same time to the same mother.

mats: clumps of knotted or tangled hair or fur in an animal's coat.

purebred/pedigree: having parents that are the same breed.

vaccinations: injections, or shots, of medicine-like substances that help fight off serious diseases.

More Books to Read

Me and My Pet Rabbit
Christine Morley and
Carole Orbell
(Two-Can)

Rabbits (Perfect Pets series)
Kathryn Hinds
(Marshall Cavendish)

**Rabbits, Rabbits, & More
Rabbits** Gail Gibbons
(Holiday House)

**Welcome to the World of Rabbits
and Hares**
Diane Swanson
(Carlton Books)

Web Sites

House Rabbit Society: Kids
www.rabbit.org/kids/

KV's Bunny Site
www.geocities.com/
kvsbunnysite/

Rabbits Online
www.rabbitsonline.com

ShowBunny
www.showbunny.com

To find additional web sites, use a reliable search engine, such as www.yahooligans.com, with one or more of the following keywords: **bunny rabbit, rabbit care, rabbits.**

Index